GREEK MYTHOLOGY

ZEUS

BY HEATHER C. HUDAK

CONTENT CONSULTANT
BILL BECK, PhD
ASSISTANT PROFESSOR
DEPARTMENT OF CLASSICAL STUDIES
INDIANA UNIVERSITY

Kids Core

An Imprint of Abdo Publishing
abdobooks.com

abdobooks.com

Published by Abdo Publishing, a division of ABDO, PO Box 398166, Minneapolis, Minnesota 55439. Copyright © 2022 by Abdo Consulting Group, Inc. International copyrights reserved in all countries. No part of this book may be reproduced in any form without written permission from the publisher. Kids Core™ is a trademark and logo of Abdo Publishing.

Printed in the United States of America, North Mankato, Minnesota.
102021
012022

THIS BOOK CONTAINS RECYCLED MATERIALS

Cover Photo: Shutterstock Images
Interior Photos: IMG Stock Studio/Shutterstock Images, 4–5, 28 (top); Shutterstock Images, 6, 10, 12–13, 16, 18, 24, 28 (bottom); NTL Studio/Shutterstock Images, 7; iStockphoto, 8, 20–21, 22, 25, 29 (bottom); The Picture Art Collection/Alamy, 14; Marvin Kochanski/Shutterstock Images, 15; Sipley/ClassicStock/Alamy, 26, 29 (top)

Editor: Alyssa Sorenson
Series Designer: Ryan Gale

Library of Congress Control Number: 2021941512

Publisher's Cataloging-in-Publication Data

Names: Hudak, Heather C., author.
Title: Zeus / by Heather C. Hudak
Description: Minneapolis, Minnesota : Abdo Publishing, 2022 | Series: Greek mythology | Includes online resources and index.
Identifiers: ISBN 9781532196812 (lib. bdg.) | ISBN 9781098218621 (ebook)
Subjects: LCSH: Zeus (Greek deity)--Juvenile literature. | Mythology, Greek--Juvenile literature. | Gods, Greek--Juvenile literature.
Classification: DDC 292--dc23

CONTENTS

CHAPTER 1
King of the Gods 4

CHAPTER 2
Rise to Power 12

CHAPTER 3
Almighty Zeus 20

Legendary Facts 28
Glossary 30
Online Resources 31
Learn More 31
Index 32
About the Author 32

Zeus is perhaps the most well-known Greek god.

CHAPTER **1**

KING OF THE GODS

Zeus was the son of a mighty Titan named Cronus. Cronus was the king of the Titans. One day, Zeus and his siblings decided to overthrow their father. The war lasted ten years.

Some artwork shows the Titans as large creatures.

Zeus got the upper hand when he asked the **cyclopes** for help. They made Zeus a powerful thunderbolt. They gave some of his siblings weapons too. Poseidon got a trident. Hades got a helmet that made him invisible.

Zeus and his siblings won the war. Then Zeus imprisoned the Titans. He put them in a deep pit in the underworld. Zeus became the king of the gods.

Zeus's Family Tree

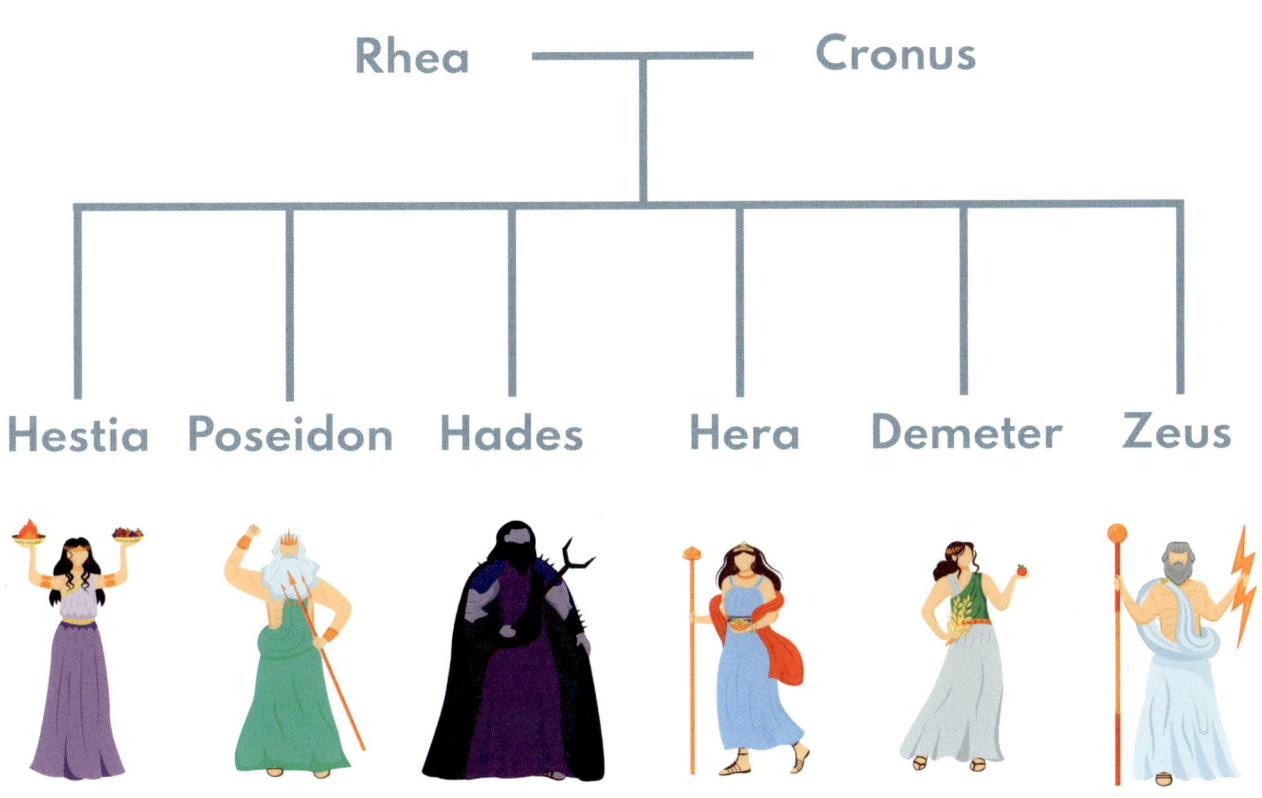

Zeus's parents, Cronus and Rhea, had six children. They were all gods and goddesses. Zeus was the youngest.

Ancient Greeks believed the gods could help them in times of war.

Greek Mythology

Ancient Greece was a **civilization** in southeastern Europe. It existed more than

2,000 years ago. The ancient Greeks believed in many gods and goddesses. Each one had different powers. People prayed to the gods. They believed the gods would help and protect them in times of need. They also thought the gods could punish them.

Ancient Greece

Some people living in ancient Greece worked as farmers, fishers, or traders. Others had jobs as soldiers and artists. The weather in Greece was warm and dry, just like it is today. Greek cities had **temples** to worship the gods. These temples often had statues and large stone columns.

Today, people in Greece can still see the remains of some ancient temples.

Ancient Greeks built **temples** to honor the gods. The Greeks told **epics** about them. The stories and legends about the Greek gods, heroes, and monsters are called Greek mythology. Some myths helped teach people meaningful lessons. Others described how the world was created and why things happened the way they did. Zeus is one of the most important gods in Greek mythology. He ruled over both gods and humans.

Further Evidence

Look at the website below. Does it give any new evidence to support Chapter One?

Ancient Greece

abdocorelibrary.com/zeus

Mount Olympus was an important site for the ancient Greeks.

CHAPTER 2

RISE TO POWER

Some stories say Zeus lived in a cave as a child. He was raised by **nymphs**. He moved to Mount Olympus when he became the king of the gods. He was one of 12 Greek gods who lived there.

Zeus and several other Greek gods were known as the Olympians. Zeus was the most powerful of them all.

Zeus and his siblings had different jobs. Poseidon was the god of horses, earthquakes, and the sea. Hades controlled the underworld. People went there after they died. Zeus ruled over the sky and controlled the weather. He could make lightning, thunder, wind, and rain.

Poseidon's name means "lord of the earth."

Some stories say Zeus threw his thunderbolt at enemies.

Zeus was also a protector. He watched over both gods and humans. He made laws and rules for them to follow. Zeus could see everything that happened from his throne on Mount Olympus. He rewarded people who did good things. He punished those who acted badly or betrayed him. The thunderbolt was his strongest weapon.

Mount Olympus

Mount Olympus is the highest mountain in Greece. Ancient Greeks believed the gods lived in a special place at the mountain's peak. It was hidden from view by clouds. People believed Zeus's throne was there.

Punishing Gods and Humans

Zeus was not always well liked. One story talks about how some of the gods tried to overthrow him. They wanted to tie him up and steal his thunderbolt. But he was rescued. Zeus punished the gods.

Another time, Zeus looked down on mankind from Mount Olympus. He saw that humans were acting badly. He caused a huge flood. A man and a woman made a boat. They survived the flood. They made new humans from stones.

Zeus was an important figure in Greek mythology.

PRIMARY SOURCE

A Greek poet named Aratus wrote about how people worshiped Zeus:

> All the streets and all the market places of humanity are full of Zeus. Also full of him are the sea and the harbors, and everywhere we all have need of Zeus. For we are also his offspring.

Source: Robert H. Gundry. *A Survey of the New Testament*. Zondervan, 2012. 362.

Comparing Texts

Think about the quote. Does it support the information in this chapter? Or does it give a different perspective? Explain how in a few sentences.

People thought Zeus brought down thunder and lightning when he was upset.

CHAPTER 3

ALMIGHTY ZEUS

Ancient Greeks believed the gods controlled the world around them. They worshipped the gods for many reasons. They prayed to Zeus to keep them safe and watch over them. Farmers often asked Zeus for good weather.

The Temple of Olympian Zeus is one temple built to honor the king of the gods. It is in Athens, Greece.

People built **altars** to Zeus in their homes and on mountains. They also built temples to honor Zeus. One of the most important temples was in Olympia, Greece. People started building it in 470 BCE. Ruins of the temple can still be seen today. It once held a huge statue of Zeus that stood 40 feet (12 m) high. It was made from ivory and gold.

The Olympics

The ancient Olympic Games took place in Olympia every four years. The games were part of a festival honoring Zeus. People came from all over Greece to take part. The winners of athletic competitions were celebrated. The Olympic Games happen today too. However, they no longer focus on Zeus.

Some stories say Zeus's eagle was his messenger and companion.

The Many Faces of Zeus

Zeus is most often shown as an older man with long hair and a thick beard. He usually has a thunderbolt or a **scepter** in his hand. He sometimes wears a wreath of oak leaves on his head. An eagle may be at his side. But Zeus can take many forms. He can change into an animal, such as a bull or swan. He can even make himself look like another person. Zeus can also change his voice to sound like someone else.

Zeus might be best known for the thunderbolt he carries.

Today, artists imagine what the statue of Zeus in Olympia looked like.

Zeus was a big part of many Greek myths. But people still tell stories of Zeus today. *Clash of the Titans* is a Hollywood movie about Zeus. *Zeus: Master of Olympus* is a popular video game. *Zeus the Mighty* is a book series for kids. Tales of Zeus and his powers will live on for years to come.

> ### Explore Online
> Visit the website below. Does it give any new information about ancient Greece and how people honored the gods?
>
> ### 10 Facts about Ancient Greece
> abdocorelibrary.com/zeus

LEGENDARY FACTS

Zeus fought a ten-year war to become the king of the gods.

Zeus's weapon of choice was a powerful thunderbolt.

People built altars and temples to honor Zeus.

People in ancient Greece worshiped Zeus. They believed he protected them.

Glossary

altars
structures where people made burnt offerings to gods

civilization
a society that's organized and developed

cyclopes
giants who have one eye at the center of their foreheads

epics
long poems that tell stories of great adventures, events, or fictional places

nymphs
divine females who live for a long time and are connected to nature

scepter
a staff or rod carried by a ruler to show authority

temples
buildings used for worship

Online Resources

To learn more about Zeus, visit our free resource websites below.

Visit **abdocorelibrary.com** or scan this QR code for free Common Core resources for teachers and students, including vetted activities, multimedia, and booklinks, for deeper subject comprehension.

Visit **abdobooklinks.com** or scan this QR code for free additional online weblinks for further learning. These links are routinely monitored and updated to provide the most current information available.

Learn More

Braun, Eric. *Zeus*. Black Rabbit Books, 2018.

Hudak, Heather C. *Hades*. Abdo, 2022.

Hudak, Heather C. *Poseidon*. Abdo, 2022.

Index

altars, 22
Ancient Greece, 8–10, 21

Cronus, 5, 7
cyclopes, 6

epics, 10

flood, 18

Hades, 6–7, 15

Mount Olympus, 13, 17–18

nymphs, 13

Olympic Games, 23

Poseidon, 6–7, 15

scepter, 25
statues, 9, 23

temples, 9–10, 22–23
thunderbolt, 6, 17–18, 25
Titans, 5–6, 27

weather, 9, 15, 21

About the Author

Heather C. Hudak has written hundreds of books on all kinds of topics. She loves to travel when she's not writing. Hudak has visited about 60 countries. She has been to Olympia and many other ancient sites in Greece dedicated to Zeus and the Olympians.